# ACTUALLY, GET BETTER.

## YOUR GUIDE TO BETTER BASKETBALL

DEVIN POLK

# Contents

# Introduction

DO NOT read this book unless you wish to turn your basketball game around. DO NOT read any further if you do not want the TRUTH about what actually working on your skills may mean for you. This guide contains honest advice and is for those who are serious about improving in basketball, have a hunger to make a change, and realize that an edge is necessary to stand out amongst the hordes of individuals seeking to do exactly what you are attempting to do. Don't be mistaken; you are not alone, and chances are, there are those who are more determined than you feel you are at this time. If you're like most and have been playing basketball for a number of un-noteworthy years, you've picked up this book to find some sort of insight because, regardless of the time you have or haven't been putting in, regardless of the miles driven and money spent, you aren't gaining the traction to become the player you know you can become.

Why is it that you have the resources, the platform, the support, the jersey, the shoes, the accessories, the eagerness, and the goals but are not making the strides that others are making and the ones you look up to have made? Why such a disparity? By the time you have completed this book, you will be extremely clear on what has to be done to become a more effective team player and a stand-out individual basketball player. When you have reached the last page of this guide, you will know where you have wasted time and where you've been remiss. This book is for those who maybe just want to make the team but don't know what changes to make to do so. The better you get at basketball, the more fun you seem to have playing. How much enjoyment can be derived from taking improvement a step further? But to answer the above questions directly, there may be too much misplaced time. I'll elaborate.

There is a kid somewhere, between the ages of let's say 7 and17 years of age, who will wake up early Saturday morning, eat a light breakfast, and be taken to his/her basketball tournament or regular weekly games. There, he or she will play in the first game of the day, do okay, or great… then wait for her second game later that day, let's say maybe 3 hours later- also playing a solid game. Then, he/she goes back home after a hard day's work to relax and prepare for tomorrow, where she and her team will finish the weekend and tournament successfully or not. Now, did she become a better basketball player that weekend? Did she sharpen her skills other than warm-up layup drills in the 3-minute pre-game warm-up time allotted? Again, miles driven, money spent, 48 good hours not taken advantage of to her benefit. Many aspiring young athletes make the mistake of spending far more time playing in games than homing in on their weaknesses- many though they are-and strengthening those areas. Even if you are a standout amongst your team, age group, league etc., know that, at the next level, you will compete against the best of other cities and the hardest working and proven talents elsewhere.

Now, I'm not against frequent high-level competition, and if you love the sport like I do, I know how addicting being a part of the action is. I only want to bring to the forefront of your awareness and attention that practice and working on your game ARE more important than game play. If your week is flooded with continuous game-time and team practice, more than likely, you will not reach your full potential as a basketball player. I hint sometimes that, when practice is over, practice isn't over. My intention is to supply you with plenty of methods and modes for you to practice effectively, so you may finally take strides in the right direction, because there are many realities pertaining to what it takes to become an elite athlete that elude the overwhelming masses.

A connotation by Malcolm Gladwell exists that has hovered around for a while, which I appreciate and believe deserves tremendous emphasis- the idea that it takes ten thousand hours of practice to master a craft. How hard this rule is, I am not positive, but it does give rise to the fact that out of 450-550 thousand high school athletes, only about 3 percent make NCAA. Of those participants, an even smaller percentage (about 1%) make it professionally. Ten thousand hours. You may consider yourself diligent and practice 7 days per week for 2.7 hour each day, and that would equal 982 hours a year. So, you need about 10 more years at that consistency to gain mastery.

Another context, if you wanted to become a mixed martial artist, and you stepped into match after match with minimal time spent sparring and practicing moves, scenarios, and situations, what would happen come fight night? You would be easily subdued, and hospitalization could be the result. That said, why do we take such an approach with our beloved sport of basketball, being that similar preparation is required?

Playing organized basketball year-round does not yield dramatic improvement. I have seen players get involved with this frequency from as early as age 7, play consistently until age 13, only to remain invisible come game time. Is this you? Have you noticed this about anyone else? A loved one maybe? Those who possess enough pride to sharpen acumen and become students of the game are the impactful players. Quite simply, they love the sport, and we, as humans, tend to donate time to what we love. Time on the training grounds when the gym is empty, and outside in the heat, wind, or rain equates to mastery. Mastery is appreciated by the masses, and those who achieve mastery are well-rewarded.

*"Under pressure you don't rise to the occasion, you sink to the level of your training."* -Chris Paul

# Part 1:
# Condition

*"I've always believed that if you put in the work, the results will come."* -Michael Jordan

Prime yourself for your Prime

# Nutrition

It's an ambition for many of us, both young and old, to grow vertically or in stature or both. Most of us would love to be in the physical condition necessary to handle circumstances as they come, regardless of difficulty. It behooves the reader of these words to consider what's necessary, not only to endure the demands of a sport as physically demanding as basketball, but to overachieve.

Imagine a high-performance car-no, imagine a race car- that was expected to perform optimally, yet it had a lower grade of fuel or little to no fuel. How well would it perform if the oil was insufficient for that type of vehicle or for what is expected of the vehicle? If we deprive a vehicle, especially of this caliber, of such care, wouldn't our expectations diminish for how we expect the race car to perform on the track?

Liken your body to a high-performance vehicle. You must put in it what's necessary to get the desired result out of it. I notice, far too often, kids and young adults hindering their development by making the simple mistake of eating too many foods that are nutritionally inopportune and neglecting themselves of and crucial sustenance and hydration that, especially if you are a child or young adult, the body is begging for.

# Heart over Height

The best teammates are those who play with the most heart. Being endowed with height won't always equate to winning, as has been proven repeatedly throughout competitive hoops by players north of 6 ft. tall, sometimes less than 6 ft. tall- but they tend to compete heavily with heart and pride. However, for those who are still within their growing phase (under 24 years of age), the amount of heart you possess when you step onto the court doesn't excuse you from doing what's in your power to grow vertically and ensure bone growth. In fact, with respect to your genetics, you may be able to determine the outcome, regarding your height, by consuming intelligently for the purpose of proper nutrition.

Kids in my neighborhood will tell you I've challenged them to drink only water and milk as beverages for the whole summer. I'm not certain how many of them actually accepted my challenge, but what I had in mind (knowing it was important to them to grow taller to be better equipped for basketball) was getting them to vitalize their growing bones with the calcium and Vitamin D they are unknowingly desperate for. As for water, like plants, we too need it to grow. My intention was hopefully to activate a growth spurt, and when properly hydrated, our bodies are fortified enough to begin to sprout.

# The Great Backcourt

I'm not referring to a dynamic guard duo, at this time, but referencing the nutrient and vitamin combo Calcium and Vitamin D that maximize growth potential. We eventually grow because our bones get bigger and longer. Calcium is of supreme importance to humans in terms of growing... To take it way back, even in the period of bone building, layers of calcium are added to cartilage, and if you didn't know, as babies, most of our bones were partly cartilage. Calcium is a building block for healthy bone development. Vitamin D is responsible for the absorption of the calcium, so as you can see, like Stockton and Malone, they work well together!  Milk (most easily accessible for most of us) in an 8-ounce glass has a nice amount of calcium, so does orange juice. Sources of Vitamin D include the sun, fish, beans, egg yolk, and orange juice. Multivitamins are great to take once a day to make sure you supplement any deficiencies from the day or the week.

# Eat

Eat. Eat three meals per day. If you've got room, snack between those meals. Reaching your growth potential requires you get to the daily recommended 2000 calories or more if you can manage to do so (the more the better). However, we shy away from 2000 good calories when we replace meals with junk food, snacks, or fillers, such as sugary soft drinks etc. While we may get full a snack pack of cookies and a bag potato chips, we've just missed an opportunity for our bodies to gain from something nutritionally valuable. So, reserve your snacking and desserts for after your meals. Don't make the mistake of replacing one eating habit with another. It's not worth it to have impaired growth as a result. I'm reminded of a kid in our neighborhood, who was rather short-too short for his age- and he was commonly asked why he was so short. He was unabashed in his response, which was that his parents never fed him enough food and vegetables, only junk food and candy- his words.

# Strengthen

The last realties you want to face when the ball is inbounded are being constantly outrun, out-jumped, outstripped, blown by, just outlasted. Assuming you agree, the term we're looking for is athletic. You want the ability to traverse the court wherever, whenever with minimal restriction. Imagine being uncontainable versus being invisible because you are constantly lagging. Athleticism demonstrating speed and agility is the goal. You too can run alongside the quick and strong, but you first need to understand why certain athletes are able to perform this way.

High-level football players are a great reference for athletes that really have it together, with physical fitness lending them certain levels of explosion and power. They are amongst the strongest athletes in all of sports; hence, they are the fastest, and some jump the highest of almost all athletes. Some say it's better to train like a football player if you want to overpower other basketball players, but they spend lots of time in the weight room and are extremely focused on the response their muscles can deliver them come *crunch* time.

Let's face it. Basketball is a running sport, where the most conditioned athletes with the stamina prevail; I'm reminded of Karl Malone, NBA Hall-of-Famer, a big guy, who was able to grab a defensive rebound, pass it off, then beat most other guys down to the other side of the court for his own basket. It was apparent that his strength and power gave him a tremendous advantage over his opponents. His prowess was unique and gave rise to his team's winning.

Our bodies have what are called slow twitching and fast twitching muscle fibers. The human body moves because of its muscles. Muscles are responsible for movement (you can tell where I'm going with this), and fast twitching muscle fibers are the largest and most powerful muscle movers in our bodies and are used for powerful bursts of movement. I'll bet you can guess which body parts are most important when it comes to picking up speed and getting up in the air. Good guess, the legs. You can target fast twitching muscle fibers in the legs by having high intensity workouts and adding resistance, or if you're older and know what you're doing, weights. If you're an adult or getting close, great, lift heavy. To this though, slowly build up week by week to heavy sets or routines and assess carefully, so you don't risk injury- safety first. You won't be running up and down the court at all with a busted knee or a torn Achilles. Target quadriceps, glutes, calves, and hamstrings prudently for an enhanced athletic delivery, so you are not reduced to only being able to carry out your intention in video games. To help in your propulsion in all directions, next is a list of exercises and drills to set you in motion.

Running Hills/ bleachers: Find a hill, set of stairs, or some bleachers that are steep enough to be moderately challenging at least. Practice proper running form. Try at least 3 sets per workout.

Speed Ladder: A must for bettering footwork, reflexes, and agility. You'll notice, the more you utilize, the faster you become. Kids love these drills, and it's a fun and effective exercise for adults as well. Do some research for simple drills and ask your coach/trainer. You can also find a hill and do some of these drills uphill.

Sprints: Long sprints and short sprints are effective. Set cones or markers 20 yards from starting point for short sprints and 60 yards for long sprints. Racing with friends adds a fun element. Remember, the best way to become a better runner is to run-a lot.

Squats: Everyone can benefit from air squats. Squats work legs in a way that promotes explosiveness and power for any athlete. If mature, add weight and safely increase if it is comfortable. Perform at least 3 sets of as many reps as possible without compromising proper form.

Suicides: Great to do with and without a ball, If you're in a group, push hard to not come in last place. Perfect to add to pre-game warm-ups.

Calf raises: Helpful for increasing vertical leap. If available, use a curb/step for full range of motion.

Lunges: Safe to do the length of a basketball court for almost any age. Focus on proper form for best results.

Pushups: Best to complete until fail- until you can no longer complete another rep. Very effective if multiple sets are completed.

Jump Rope: Count to 30, 60, or to 100. Rest and repeat. Also suitable as part of pre-game warm-up.

You can challenge yourself by timing some of these drills and keeping track of your times, always striving to improve.

# Part 2:

# Becoming an Offensive Threat

*"I was always in the gym. People would look at me crazy because I spent so much time there. But that's what it was about. I'm glad I did it."* -Kevin Durant

Can you honestly claim that you pose a threat on offense? Does it seem that you are victimizing defenses? Does the audience look at your every move in anticipation? Do you shift the momentum of the game when your number is called? This section is dedicated to helping you answer yes to these questions, and if you already do, then let's make it a yes with an exclamation point.

When asked by players, coaches, and parents how to turn around their basketball output, I'm tempted to state the obvious and be old-fashioned and suggest they practice every day. Practicing every day is a sure way to get where you want to be, but beyond that, practice the right way. How to make your practice effective is the question. How do you *ensure* you're growing in your craft and take the best approaches? Let's put our progress under a microscope to see why some of us are more precise than others or the reason some of us are seemingly *naturals,* while others struggle.

# What is Skill?

What is skill? How does it work? And how do we add layers to skill sets? The following sections and the remainder of this guide give recipes to transform a player at any stage in development into a more potent and well-rounded offensive threat, but what is occurring biologically within ourselves that leads to this improvement? Before diving into your newfound maddening training regimens, understand what skill *really* is. Understand what occurs within that's causing you to be more reflexive and responsive, versus when you began your journey. When you picked up a basketball for the first time, it felt as if you had five thumbs. Then, something happened to sharpen you.

A more scientific look at skill is the understanding of the function of something termed *Myelin*. Myelin can be described as the substance wrapped around our nerve fibers increasing the speed of our impulses. Note that every action we take and habit we carry out is computed in the brain, which signals our muscles to act specifically.

These signals travel to our neurons as fast as 200 or more miles per hour via electrical impulses similar to electrical wiring. Furthermore, Myelin, insulates and protects the nerve fibers, so the signals can transmit more rapidly or so you can react more quickly and be more precise when doing anything. This white matter can wrap around your nerve fibers thickly. Actually, the more a nerve fiber is myelinated, the better you are at whatever the task at hand may be. The more insulation the nerve fiber has, the faster the signal strength and speed- and accuracy. As you know, we have developed several skills in life, writing, reading, jumping rope, dancing, dribbling a basketball, shooting a free throw etc. Myelin is made, and skill is formed. Myelin equals skill; this is the easiest way to understand it. To be simplistic, electrical signals fire between neurons, but myelin makes the signals fire more efficiently (remember the myelin sheath you learned about in school). Learning connections are formed in the brain at all ages and never stop; anyone at any age can become more skillful, but myelin sheaths enable your brain to send these signals much, much faster. But how is it formed?

Myelin layering is formed by doing a thing over and over again or practicing. This is why it's important to do what you love every day or as often as possible because, when you do so/have done so, you will notice the ease in execution, let's say, of backing out of the driveway or out of a parking space, in comparison to completing that complicated set of steps for the first time when you began learning to drive. Backing out of the driveway is no easy task for the average person the first time. Its complexity requires you to be attentive and to take your time. Then, after having to back out of parking spaces every day for a couple of years, the action is no longer tasking in the slightest. The same can be said for a reverse layup or anything else within basketball. Repetition and frequent practice leads to adding Myelin to increase skill, and you can add myelin indefinitely until you are unerring and near perfection and onward to specific practices for well-pronounced attributes as an elite ball player.

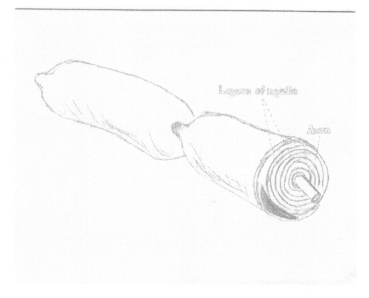

# The Shot

*"My best move is probably my pull up jump shot."*-Steve Nash

Having an effective jump-shot is instrumental for an offensive threat. You may be a great ball handler, but if you can't knock down open shots, wiser defenders and opposing coaches will give you space to absorb your first step no matter how quick you are and will be able to afford to do so because of your ineffective shooting. Conversely, there are players, who can go on a scoring spree with very few dribbles and keep a defense/defender at bay. The defense is always forced to respect a good shooter.

Adding shooting ability to your game opens up and diversifies your offense and turns you into a more attractive player.

It is a lengthy journey to pure shooting, especially at first. It's puzzling to see other players seem to score from a distance at-will, while you are shooting 'at' the basket. A couple things to ease your worries- primarily, once you do enough shooting, then eventually making, you will improve your aim. You can eventually get comfortable at any distance. Simply stated, great shooting comes through repetition and practice, like improvement in anything else. Second, making a jump-shot is far easier than it lets on from the average observer's perspective. In fact, when a shot is swished in, I suppose it's considered that the shot was made with perfect aim. However, this is actually not the case. You don't have to be perfect; you just have to be close. Let's elaborate.

Future sharp shooters should first understand that the rim is much larger than the basketball. In fact, you would be relieved to know two regulation size basketballs can fit inside the rim at the same time. The fact that the hoop is twice the size of the ball you may be stressing about or feel anxiety over getting through should be received like a breath of fresh air. It may be helpful, if possible, to go out and see for yourselves. I've included an image to show this, but it may serve as an extremely helpful object lesson for you to go out and physically see for yourself (of course, you'd have to lower the court safely in your back or front yard to a reachable height). A men's size regulation basketball is about 9 inches in diameter, while a regulation size rim is 18 inches in diameter (9x2=18). The balls have to be side by side and enter through the rim simultaneously to fit and is possible only if entered straight from above (as if dropped or placed downward right through it).

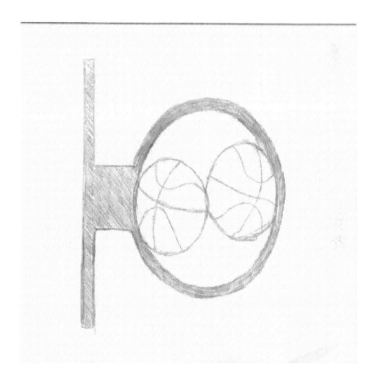

## The Power of Arch

The key word there is "downward", meaning the balls were dropped or placed through from above. Aside from knowing the rim is wide enough to fit 2 basketballs should make the task of making baskets much less daunting, soon-to-be shooters should also be aware of the efficiency of an arc on the basketball when shooting. If the ball - we're talking about one ball now- drops through the net directly from above or "downward," the entry angle would be considered 90-degrees and the result will be a swish in the middle of the inside of the rim. The goal then should be to get as close to this 90 degree as possible, so the more arc you put or add to your shot, the closer to the 90-degree you would get, thus enhancing your efficiency. More arc = higher shooting percentage. Within this simplified breakdown of a proper jump-shot, it's the last detail in my shot mechanics that I suggest to my players- toes, square, put it in the air...*putting it in the air* means have arch; we'll go over toes and square very soon here. This will change things for the aspiring shot maker, so now for a deeper look.

We referenced the fact that 90 degrees is a perfect scenario for the end of the *trajectory* on your shot, but it's not very common. It's unrealistic and unnatural. What we do notice is a ball release at 35-degrees, for example, which is a rather *flat* shot, meaning it has very little arc. A shot this flat only has a .6 margin for the ball to clear without hitting rim. In this case, you have to have nearly perfect aim for it to go in the basket. However, if you increase the arch slightly in this example to 45 percent -just 10 percent more- you give yourself a 3-inch margin of error. Mathematics are involved here, but for emphasis, it's an increase in margin of error of roughly 500%. Again, the more arch, the better chances of the ball dropping through. Although there is more involved, I often tell players that I personally coach, depending on their stage in development, that arch is the most important part of a shot.

One of the best professional players to shoot the ball, Stephen Curry, tends to release the basketball between a 50 and 55% angle. The important thing to note here is that he doesn't depend entirely on aim, but also adds *height* to his shot, giving him tremendous advantage and utilizing the power of arch. When Stephen Curry shoots a ball, it actually reaches a higher point IN THE AIR than other professional players on average. Could this, along with his incredible work ethic, be behind his incredible fluidity in shooting the ball? As for work ethic, I've heard that Curry during off-season makes 500 shots per day and 2-300+ during the season. Is it a mystery that he has done some of the things he has done for the game with that type of implementation? No. It's easy to state that he's reached amazing heights and a multitude of accomplishments, and this easily stands out in one of the biggest attributes of his game among many.

# Technique and Shot Mechanics

Rather than throwing the basketball at the rim like a football, of course, there's a proper way to fine tune yourself so a shot is more likely to splash in. Without shot mechanics, there would be a huge difference in the way each player takes a shot, but through identifying what works best in gameplay over time, a standard approach is taken, hence the modern way a shot is taken today. Eventually, you should want your shot to release high (high release), and at the end and peak of your jump -or close to it, make a wrist snap as the ball leaves your fingertips. This is the grossly simplified description of good shooting form and how it's executed.

Regarding shot mechanics, a name comes to mind, one that happens to have a meticulous checklist for his shot release. He has, to-date, the single season 3-point percentage high at 53 percent in the NBA-Kyle Korver. Interestingly, his last name means, in German, basketmaker. At the time he achieved this milestone of making over half of the shots he was taking from almost 24 feet away, there were only a dozen NBA players making shots at that percentage inside the arc-he must've been onto something- what separates him?

Korver, who states he was never a basketball prodigy and that he simply had to work and earn his way, has a 20-point mental checklist:

- Wide stance
- Exaggerate legs
- Drop through heels
- Slight bend at waist
- Engage Core
- Up Strong
- Straight Elbow
- One Hand
- Spread Fingers
- Slight Pause
- Elbow up
- Land Forward
- See top of Rim
- Use fingertips
- Strong shot
- shoulders Forward
- Ball and arm rise straight
- Hold Follow through
- High Release
- On turns, square shoulders

Whew, that's somewhat extensive, but we are referring to a record holder and former NBA all-star. Is it worth it? If that's what worked for him to reach the heights he has, then I'd bet his answer would be "yes." He wanted to have something, elaborate though it is, he could practice and duplicate that would give him a high likelihood of scoring from long range. I imagine he spent many hours repeating shot attempts with this checklist in mind, but some of this is easily identifiable when observing him in action. You can do nothing but respect his approach. The question now is, do YOU have a set checklist that you practice over and over, so you are ready for your shot opportunity? Have you even sought one? I think it's time you did.

# Basics

What most stands out to me in a correct shot form and follow-through are only a handful of details. I advise to have a strong balanced foundation (the legs). You always want to set your feet slightly apart and be balanced and shoot on your toes. Notice that, when you see anyone shoot with consistent accuracy, there is space between their heel and the ground; there are shooting almost *tip-toed*. If, for example, you are a *right* hand shooter, always have your *right* foot or toe pointed to the center of the basket and *ahead* of your left foot, *never* behind your left foot. Also, let's emphasize the *jump* in j*ump shot* but be sure to bend your knees and execute a balanced jump straight upward.

The second necessity in a shot is a strong *back*. This is simple; don't arch your lower back or bring your shoulders forward if you can help it. Rather, keep your elbows back, as if you have Superman's "S" on your chest.

Pay close attention to your *arms* in your shooting form. This seems obvious, but we notice some shooters that don't have their elbow under the ball when it's about to be released. This cannot make for consistent good aim and is not as easy to duplicate. The inexperienced shooter is easy to spot. They usually shoot flatfooted (not on their toes), and their elbow is pointed outward, rather than in the direction of basket/target area. So, without making it too uncomfortable, start taking practice shots with your shot arm closer to your body, and your aim should gradually improve.

# Mr. Hopla

With hopes of increasing shot accuracy, I thought it might be helpful to talk about some of the insights of the best shooting coach in the world, Dave Hopla. Mr. Hopla is also known for setting a world record for most NBA 3 pointers made in under 1 minute using one ball and one passer (18). He's worked with several NBA teams and players, teams including the Pistons, Knicks, Raptors and Wizards to name a few, and has given personal advice and coaching to the likes of Kobe Bryant and Ray Allen. When he hosts clinics for shooting around the world, in demonstrations, he usually makes close to 100 percent of his shots.

Something I have implemented in my coaching is his advice to visualize the *swish*. He states that the only thing he is concerned about mentally is the center of the basket. Each time he gives a shot attempt, he is thinking "swish," nothing else, As he says, "Shots are made before they're taken."

Dave Hopla also stresses correct and disciplined shooting form. Making more shots than everyone else involved him taking more *correct* shots than everyone else. *Always starting close and working his way out* in his shooting warm-ups, and as other great shooters are known to demonstrate, he focuses on his shooting arm, keeping his elbow straight. I've noticed, in his shooting warm-ups, he warms up with his shooting arm only or one arm shots. He is sharpening his shooting form up close then gradually further from the basket and releasing the ball high, which lends to his statement that: if you *minimize motion*, you increase accuracy.

A great detail to keep in mind with what we're discussing is the habit of *starting close* and working your way out (further and further from the basket). I can't emphasize the importance of this enough as this will save you a lot of time in your shooting workout. Too often I witness shot takers walk onto the court to practice, and begin with long range shots rather than closer to the basket. You'll be able to have a far more effective and efficient workout, as you'll familiarize yourself with the basket early.

This shot making expert frequently remarks that, *good* is the enemy to *great*, and the difference between good and great is the time one puts in. Once you manage to get a good shooting form, you need to practice "obsessively," as he puts it. Obsessive, a characteristic both Ray Allen and Kobe Bryant possessed before requesting his coaching, they were perfect students.

*"I aim for the center of the basket every time."* -Dave Hopla

# Approach

Expectation: Be prepared to dedicate yourself to becoming a sharp shooter. This means the dedication of time and much of it. Be prepared to be taking shots, sometimes until you are bored of it or until your shoulders feel heavy. DO NOT make the mistake of thinking your shot will improve without time. You cannot cheat the hours required for good jump-shooting, 3-point hitting, or high percentage free-throw shooting. The purpose of this guide, of course, is to see that your time working out and practicing is spent efficiently to reach the destination faster. I would be remiss if I didn't mention there will be lots of frustration from fine tuning, changing certain habits, chasing rebounds (less chasing will be necessary, once you start to get the hang of it and find something that works), lack of results early on, criticism etc.

I have said, on occasion, to those just starting that all the pros miss roughly the same amount of shots from the time they first embark on their journey to when they reach an elite level, and it's the ones that don't care as much about the misses and keep going that get where they're going.

The benchmark you want to reach is 10/10 (or more) when you're putting in shots at practice or without defense or anyone guarding you. Hopefully, you have reached the dedication level at this point and are willing to do what it takes to reach 10/10, probably at least 200 makes or more per day. I should mention that 10/10 also applies to beyond the arc, so if you have a penchant for firing from behind the 3-point line, strive for 10 out of 10 there, as well, as you develop.

# Rebounder

As often as you can, have someone or a friend rebound your makes and misses for you. Some call it *spotting*, as in, "Hey, can you *spot* me for 20 shots?" If you have a trainer, likely, they already render this invaluable service, as it saves lots of time and allows you to focus primarily on your shot form and follow-through. Imagine how helpful it would be to work on catching and shooting at game speed, rather than chasing down your own rebounds and walking away from the target area on the court you're trying to master. Too infrequently, I see two friends or teammates or family members implement a sort of buddy system and trade off *spotting* one another, which increases the amount of practice shot attempts and decreases the amount of time it would normally take to make them.

# Legs

Don't be fooled by fresh legs. You'll be able to shoot better if your legs aren't tired and you haven't undergone any fatigue. Do you agree that most can hit a shot more easily early in the game, as opposed to when the score is close and time is winding down? That is because we need our legs to power our jump shooting. It's much more difficult to garner balance necessary for a jumper if you have been sprinting up and down the court and applying heavy defense on your opponent for 30 minutes. There is a saying that goes: "practice how you play," which is why it's critical to run in your workout, give your legs some burn, make sure they are warm before or during a shooting workout, so muscle memory can correctly play its role in real situations.

Example: Exercise legs if there's time before shooting practice by jump-roping, running suicides, short sprints, defensive slides, performing lunges, calf raises, sprints etc.

Implementation of this strategy makes for a more *realistic* shooting practice.

# The work

*"God will give you a lot of things in life, but he's not going to give you your jump shot. Only hard work will give you that."* - Ray Allen

The following information is less of a tip and more of a prescription for those willing to move forward with certainty in the endeavor of becoming a pure shooter. As indicated earlier, developing a stroke requires much work ethic. The level of your commitment will be tested by how seriously you take the following formulas. As a coach and a trainer, I've suggested this outlook as a method and have seen it work multiple times. I've even tested it myself. Now that we have a mutual understanding of how important the shot form is, going forward, we'll utilize your new way of shooting and put up some numbers.

75 makes per day- ok shooter

150 makes per day-  good shooter

200+ makes per day- great shooter

Try it.

Granted, getting up to these numbers will take some time because you'll probably be adjusting to a new and improved shooting form, and you'll have a lot of misfires early on in your journey. The upside to all your work is that, once you start improving, you will be increasingly valuable to your team(s), something every hooper would like to become.

Imagine this scenario. You're in an offensive half court possession, and the ball is moving around with purpose to the dismay of the defense; however, they are making a solid defensive stance. A ball handler and/or you attempted to cause some penetration closer to the basket but were unable to. Frustration is setting in. The half-court defense of the opposing team is wearing down your offense, but as usual, with enough ball movement...the defense collapses eventually somewhere. The defense has a lapse, and you get a semi-open shot from long range; you take it, and just as you've practiced, it splashes through.

Shots such as this are deflating to defenses. In this example, the wind was temporarily knocked out of the opposing team. You knocked the wind out of them given your ability to make an open shot -greatly appreciated by your teammates and your coach. It's a good thing you practiced catching and shooting several hundred times last week. I've asked some of my trainees if the work was worth it, to be able to make open jumpers when the opportunity presents itself; the answer's always a glad yes.

# Bundles

Something became apparent to me from observing someone that I trained and coached, as they were competing over the span of a few games. Our player/ trainer relationship was in its infancy. They had only worked out with me a few times, and it seemed that their jump shot was somewhat streaky. Even though they had put up a couple hundred makes with me during our workout, the results I was expecting weren't yielding as I planned. Granted, they had improved their shot making noticeably, but not to my expectation. Seeking an answer, amongst other things, I began to look at the amount of makes one would make *in a row*. I paid attention to this detail for a few of my players, and what was being revealed was that, along with the increased makes daily, the third and fourth make in a row was more closely related to a game make.

This finding is worth emphasis and has been a more concrete measurement for progress. Again, the third and/ or fourth make *in a row*, -that's one make, 2 in a row, 3 in a row during practice- will be more like your game shot, so you also need to be counting the number of *bundles* of 3 made when you work on your jumper.

Example, today, a partner or my trainer and I worked on perimeter shots. I made a total of 250 three-pointers. Taking mental notes, which I later wrote down (I always log my work done that day), I was able to make 3 in a row 10 times at least, and 5 in a row 7 times, and 10 in a row twice. In that example, I made 10 bundles of 3, 7 bundles of 5, and 2 bundles of 10.

Eventually, you'll be able to drop in many more than three in a row as time progresses and you keep consistent. At the same time, as your streaks of makes are increasing, your in-game shooting should also increase in consistency. An important thing to keep in mind, days and weeks after days and weeks of training jumpers, please keep a good form, something that is easily duplicated in real time and game time speed. With your newfound form or release that is hopefully much more efficient, strive for a perfect 10 for 10 or more (bundles of 10) as often as possible.

This isn't to say that hitting 10 for 10 in practice or a workout will translate to 10 for 10 during the game. However, it is possible that 10 for 10, come practice time for good shooters, could translate to 5 or 6 for 10 during the game (50%). Being able to make a bundle of 10 or 15 or more (100%), during workouts, *is no*t to be confused with 7 or 8 or 9 for 10 in your workout. The mental focus necessary for that 9th and 10th+ make in a row is more closely related to a game make.

Remember, implement running in your shooting workout to simulate what your legs will feel like come game time.

# The Handle

*"My focus is basketball, and that's it."* - Kyrie Irving

There is a pronounced distinction between dribbling and ball handling. Dribbling a basketball can be achieved by a 3-year-old who is picking up the ball for the first time. You can picture it, sort of patting at the ball; the ball and the child have about equal say as to where the ball is heading. Ball handling is just that, *handling* the ball with control and intention. The idea is to go wherever necessary on the court, at will, despite how stubborn the defense is. From now on, rather than dribbling the ball, without much resolve, you will shift to a player that handles the basketball well.

Other sports, namely hockey and soccer, require its professionals to have an excellent handle as well. These professionals and would-be outstanding players certainly did not begrudge the time it took to make the handle look easy and perform up to par competitively amongst other great athletes. With this in mind, ask yourself, what is a true hooper without good ball control? Notice, most "big men" in the league do less ball handling during the game, yet they still possess a respectable handle for any scenario that might arise. That being said, every serious basketball hopeful need not overlook skilled ball control as an attribute worth obtaining and developing, regardless of position or size.

## Become Ambidextrous

Having worked with many younger athletes and beginners, a commonality among them happens to be their habit of driving the ball down the right side of the court into the corner. Starting out, most children have only developed their right hand. All they aim to do is get to the right side of the basket for a close enough shot. Eventually, 9 times out of 10, they get trapped somewhere along the right side, and the ball barely makes it out if at all. If you're a newer basketball parent, you know exactly what I'm talking about. Things don't have to be this way, though. From the start, we have to start teaching them to use both hands evenly in training and practice. The sooner they get the hang of utilizing both sides of the court, the better the team will fare, the better they will fare. So then, all drills etcetera need to include both hands, and every move taught, if applicable, both directions. Good basketball uses both sides of the court; thus, good ball handlers don't have weakness in either direction.

# One on One

When I was in middle school, one day after school, I indelibly lost a game of one on one to a guy. I do not remember who he was or where he came from, as our school courts were open to the public after the bell rang to go home, but we battled going up to 13, and though I played hard and did what was my best at the time... I fell short and lost. I remember being heartbroken and even had slight tears from the loss. I usually was able to overcome other guys through athleticism alone, but not this time. I lost by a couple of points and was not the better player this time around. This loss was painful, to say the least, and I absolutely hated losing, especially in the sport I loved most. However, I did learn two things that afternoon. The first lesson was that I was not as good as I thought I was, and second, I didn't want to lose again as long as I played basketball.

I obsessed over what made me lose to this other guy and worked at my weaknesses, resolute to turn them into strengths. If I had the opportunity, I would go out, by myself preferably, and work at my shortcomings until they became strong-suits. I wanted to make sure that, the next time I played one on one, I'd win, period, and I did...from that day forward. Shortcomings to strong-suits, would seem to most to be commonsense, but, common sense isn't always common practice. One can train, attend practice etc., but it's difficult to gauge the way the skills you learned would work out when you're being defended. Going head to head with another player is a great way to test how proficient your ball handling is when you have a defender concentrating on you. Here is a great opportunity to test what works and what doesn't and what's necessary versus what isn't. So many players repeat the same ineffectual dribbling habits when they are not useful. Playing one on one is a service to yourself as you learn your limitations and your capacity for creating space and/or getting to the basket. Remember, with competition as heavy as it is, it's imperative to get any and every edge you can get over all the other people trying to get to the same place you are. One on one costs nothing; it's *free*. You can play at a park, with anyone...you're only helping one another improve in some way, as defeat is a teacher, and failures are lessons. I challenge you to go out, challenge as many people as you can, so you may learn what your identity is as a basketball player and determine which areas you can expand upon.

# Whoever is Lower Wins

When attacking the basket, seizing opportunities to advance closer toward your basket, or simply shaking defenders off you, it's best practice to be lower than they are, or as I commonly phrase it, "whoever's lower wins." This actually applies to defensive positioning as well, but we won't tell your opponents that. The ball has to come up from the ground to your dribbling hands, so you want to have a closer relationship to your ball than everyone else by maintaining a low, tight dribble when necessary to protect the possession. Simple logic, right? If the defender has a higher stance and yours is much lower, they will need to adjust more dramatically in their upright position to keep in front of you as you maneuver where you need to score etc. If they risk and attempt to go for a steal or take the ball from you in some way, you'd be requiring them to lunge downward, something the defense isn't comfortable doing. If a defender tries to steal from you but misses, there will likely be a misstep, providing you with your pathway free or forward. Keep in mind center of gravity, the area around the belly button. Ensure that your center of gravity is lower than your opponent's when applicable. As I say, *"put your chest on the ground,"* which means to make your chest parallel to the floor. Center of gravity, this has a lot to do with one's ability to guard another, and the goal is to strip every one of their propensity to keep you from doing what you'd like to do on the court.

## Prey on the weak

Know your advantages over others. Press your advantages, and intend to expand your advantages over a broader range of competition over time. So yes, prey on the weak, which may be very few right now, but with practice and training and the progression of time, you'll notice you have abilities that make your competition seem weaker and weaker. For example, by developing your ball handling to the point that you're more shifty and difficult to guard, you might find that the mediocre defenders that could keep up with you before are now much too slow to react.

Keep in mind that defense is a reaction disposition. They are essentially reacting to what you are doing and the move you made a split-second prior. Their goal is to stay in front of you, prevent you from advancing, and sometimes anticipate what you may do. This is where creativity comes in. At times, you'll need to be somewhat crafty and elusive. These are player characteristics that are developed through practice.

Habitually isolate yourself and work on moves and changing direction etc. with no one in front of you. Use imagination and practice the way you might break free of a defender, so you can implement that scenario later if it arises. As I'll list later as a useful practice method, find a mirror or something that reveals your reflection, so you can see what you look like as you make certain moves or move a specific way- you might be surprised at what you see. You might notice what you should continue doing or something in particular that doesn't look as sharp as it feels when you are performing the move. If you look at your reflection or even a recording of yourself free-styling with your ball, you can note how sharp you look. The more acuity you have with handling the ball in various ways, the harder it will be for defenders to react and do their job. When you observe yourself, ask, would *I* be able to guard myself? Adjust accordingly. Essentially, remember, you want the ball to feel like a part of your hand or an extension of your arm.

# Be Fake

At every position, it's critical that you be deceptive with the basketball. Whoever guards you should be constantly guessing incorrectly as to what you might do next. As the game progresses, the other team will become familiar with and adapt to your style of play and try to anticipate you at times if they're confident enough. You might have to do something different than you have been doing if you find yourself struggling to free yourself or get enough space to score. The reality is, you have to be shifty and unpredictable, especially at the guard/forward positions. Judge yourself to determine the typical difficulty players have keeping you from scoring. Chances are, you have work to do.

## Key Moves

*"What I want fans to realize is that when I make a move, it's really a simple move, it's just done with pace, and it's done off a counter of something. I only do those moves when someone kind of puts me in that position. When someone makes me feel uncomfortable, I'll always have a change of pace or have a change of direction to kind of keep them off balance. They can only guess, so you're in control. That's what offensive guys need to remember."* -Kyrie Irving

Focus heavily on developing the following fundamental maneuvers to enhance/expand offensive performance.

# Crossover

The general basketball definition for a crossover is simply a change of direction while changing the ball from one hand to the other. Essentially, you want the defender, for example, to guess that you're going right, yet you're actually going the other way. You want the defender out of your way, so you can drive to the basket or get them off-balance, so you can pass shoot or get closer to the basket. Best results are had when your crossover is convincing. The best ball-handlers and offense of threats have a variety of crossovers and one main crossover that is likely to have its desired effect.

This maneuver can be predictable, especially for seasoned defenders and those that are good ball-handlers; they can see one coming from a mile away. *Low and wide* are the makings of a good crossover and certainly one that is quick, which is why you have to carve out time to work specifically on crossover(s) that work for you.

# Jab Step

Upon receiving a pass and naturally with the defender in front of you, jab steps are for causing the person guarding you to think you will start your possession of the basketball going one way or another, without actually using a dribble but, of course, maintaining a pivot foot. As it is with everything in basketball, this is worth a little practice, as a successful enough jab-step can shake your man off you, especially if you use their defensive momentum against them.

# Behind-the-Back

Worthy of being the favorite it is, the behind-the-back dribble is one of the most elusive options you have to lose a defender. For the defensive player, it's difficult to gauge the ball-handler's momentum and the direction you're headed with the ball simultaneously. Also, it's extremely costly to reach for the ball and attempt to steal it as you handle a ball hidden (bouncing) behind your back. You would be remiss not include and to skip this facet of ball handling, which would make you that much more difficult to guard. Definitely dedicate time to this one and watch your offensive game open up by adding crafty behind the back dribbling (used carefully) to your arsenal of offensive weapons.

## In and Out Dribble

Similar to a crossover, only the ball is never transferred to the other hand. Think of it as a one-handed crossover, in which you briefly and very quickly glance in the direction you are faking. Another move that works best when executed lower to the ground than your defender, as the goal is to render them somewhat off-balance in the opposite direction you actually intend on heading. When performing almost every dribble move, remember that your knee on the leg you are leading with will tell the defender where you are going, so for the In-and-out, step with the foot opposite the side the ball is dribbled on, in the direction you want to fake. It's a great move to make in the half court but even more effective on the full court breakaway/fast break situations.

## Pump Fake Head Fake

For avoiding the shot block and creating room to complete the desired shot attempt, it is also effective in getting a feel of how they are defending you, in a way, sizing up the defender. It can be utilized to free yourself from a defender in a variety of ways, including but certainly not limited to:

-Upon catching a pass. If sold well enough, the defender may leave their feet for a shot block, leading to a wide-open shot, shot closer to the basket, a pass for a better shot etc.

or

-Off the dribble using a head fake *in conjunction* with bringing your *threat-to-shoot* hand toward the basketball.

*Eye contact* with the basket or toward the basket is critical when selling your pump fake. The player guarding you or closing out your shot attempt must believe you want to take that shot in hopes of covering or deflecting the shot attempt (shot block).

# The Work

*"I trained for 5-6 hours daily as a kid. My Father would have me do all sorts of drills every day. I followed his teachings and it is one of the main reasons why I have succeeded in my life."*
-"Pistol" Pete Maravich

Drills/workout tips

2 ball dribbling- Used by beginners and those learning to develop coordination with both hands at once and used by experienced ball handlers to keep sharp and ensure the ball is an extension of the hand during gameplay. 2-ball workout segments include dozens of different challenging drills that make handling the basketball second nature. For example, jog laps around a full court bouncing two basketballs at once (one in each hand) or run full court suicides bouncing a basketball in each hand. Ask your trainer/coach or visit the web for variations of these effective drills, as they can never be overused.

Tennis Ball drills- Meant to enable you to dribble with little-to-no thought. You can put down your basketball and simply pretend a tennis ball is a basketball and handle it as such. Obviously, handling a tennis ball as if it were a basketball requires much more attention and requires more sensitivity in the hands. Another easy to learn drill with the tennis ball, you can pick up your basketball, dribble in a triple threat positioning, toss a tennis ball up with the hand that doesn't dribble the basketball, and catch the tennis ball with the same hand. To simplify, you are dribbling with one hand, while the other tosses up a tennis ball and catches the tennis ball. Be sure to switch hands. Ask your trainer/coach or visit the web for variations of this drill.

Repetition- For the simplest actions in ball handling, from "*kill*" or "*pounding*" the ball (a rapid dribble on either left or right side using the corresponding hand while in your triple threat position) to dribbling between the legs in stationary positioning in either direction (right or left). Of course, there are several dribble moves to use with this practice, but the idea is to continue that dribble for at least 30 seconds per side or dribble option, for example, a stationary behind-the-back dribble for 1 minute, or a side to side dribble with the basketball bouncing in front of you for 1 minute or whatever time frame is suitable. Try to imagine that, if every professional has bounced a basketball roughly the same amount of bounces in their lifetime, using *repetition* drills in a way helps you to catch up to where you need to be as well.

Grass Dribbling- Find a grassy area where you can practice the aforementioned *Repetition* drills or simply freestyle dribble with a basketball. Handling a basketball in turf or grass requires more strength in the hands, so it aids in muscle memory and heightens focus to keep your basketball in a controlled dribble, because the lumpier surface can drive the ball away awkwardly. I've found this to be extremely useful to the beginner ball handler.

Wrap arounds- Bring the ball to your waist and wrap it around your waist at a challenging speed for a given amount of time, 30 seconds, for example, then do the same in the other direction. You can do the same at the knee area and ankle area; just be sure to repeat in both directions (or both hands if applicable) with every drill you complete for fullest dexterity with a basketball.

Blind Fold- Notice how well you handle certain drills without visibility. Handle work is improved here by activating higher sensitivity in hands and to movements because one of your senses is not used. Reaching a point where you do not need to see the basketball, except with your mind's eye, is absolutely necessary at every level of competition. Alternatives to using a blind fold are simply closing your eyes or using dribble glasses. Dribble Glasses are glasses that have blinders that block downward vision and allow you to look only straight forward, at your sides, or upward.

Usage of Cones or Props- Referred to as *"cone work,"* cones serve as obstacles and/or cues to change/make certain moves. Adding a challenging fun spin on workout routines, they serve as a simulation of a defender before you, making the drill or workout more realistic and game-like. There are countless variations and combinations of things to try with your coaches, friends, and loved ones. Anything from trash cans to chairs can be positioned on a court or any safe area where ball handling can be practiced.

Freestyle Dribbling- Most dedicated basketball players will seem to always have a basketball in their hands. We even see some students whom if allowed, bring their ball to school with them as well as most everywhere else. With the idea in mind that every achieved hooper has a similar number of hours in their lifetime handling the ball, you should do what you can to handle the ball and work on your moves in a leisurely fashion as well. After all, there is no shortage of concrete and hard ground surrounding us.

# The Pass

*"Either you move it or you die."* - Gregg Popovich

## Ball movement

Passing is a skill that deserves and requires attention for development as a player and as a team. It doesn't come as a surprise that the best teams and those that have had the most success are the most willing passing groups.

Audiences, teams, and their coaches, no doubt, appreciate having a singular force on their team, such as a dominant guard who is seemingly unstoppable. However, it is equally, if not more, appealing and entertaining to spectators to witness teamwork and great offensive flow from ball movement within offensive possessions. After all, 5 is better than 1, and the knight, as an analogy, may be able, if he is strong enough, to slay a fierce dragon, but it's

63

nearly impossible to slay a five-headed dragon. That said, it's extremely difficult to stop a rotating ball no matter how athletic the defense is. The great equalizer of athleticism in basketball is ball movement because you can be the fastest player in the world, but you can't catch up to the ball moving around the court when done properly. It's deflating for defense to exert their best efforts as a team only to be subject to an eventual open jump shot/field goal.

What's occurring here, is more use of the whole basketball court. Defense being the reactionary disposition lends to the fact that it becomes increasingly difficult to contain a passing sequence when there is offensive penetration, rotation, and off-ball movement (back-cuts, screens, off ball screens etc.). In swinging the ball with the *intention* of finding the *most* open player, the defense will *eventually* have a lapse and breakdown somewhere, thus freeing someone up for a potential basket.

Through studying footage, I noticed, at the end of a passing sequence, there would be not *one* person open but sometimes *two* available open options for a shot attempt. Also gained from investigating footage was frustration from noticing *stagnant* offenses- too much dribbling with no advancement and little-to-no ball movement before shot attempts etc.

Someone is always open. Do not underestimate the advantages of making the extra pass. The adoption of this mindset must be had by the entire team to make their offense seem unsolvable to the opponent. The pros of having such a mentality as a whole include enhanced offensive vibe and enforcement of *trust* amongst teammates.

"When the play is broken, someone is open."

# Assists

It is more difficult to shut down an offensive player that is a distributor. They have a skill for locating the open teammate (there usually is at least one) and, if necessary, putting them in a position to score easily. They activate the rest of the offense, so they become a coach, teammate, and crowd favorite, making them a threat because they make the other teammates potential threats. The willing passer is someone that perceivably understands the game and how it's played best and most efficiently and is refreshing to play with.

On behalf of the 'big' men, who are often neglected of touches in offensive possessions, a good wing player or guard, for example, who knows where and when to give them the ball, is a treat to have on their team because they are kept involved- after all, they have a very important role on the team, as they're required to protect the basket and do most of the rebounding to begin the offense. They deserve the reward of having equal scoring opportunities.

An upside to being known for *dropping dimes* is that defense may, at times, sag off of you, some trying to anticipate and deflect because of your passing capabilities, further freeing you up for scoring of your own. However, to their dismay, you affect the scoreboard more than others. For example, you may add 10 of your own points to the scoreboard but have 10 assists on top of that. Great job, so you are more than less responsible for a total of 20 total points, which is a significant impact.

Be *that* player, who makes sharing the basketball contagious as a team. Coaches appreciate and notice when a player helps the ball move across the basketball court, as they hate stagnant offense. An assist can be a highlight too, but unfortunately, passing and instinctive passing is an undertrained skill but is certainly appreciated and beneficial once possessed.

Be deceptive. It's important to understand that, if you have the basketball in an offensive sequence, you are a diversion from the other actions and movements occurring away from the ball. The defense, and usually everyone else, is watching the ball. Their eyes are on the basketball. You have the opportunity to draw in all the attention on the court, to kick it out or dish the ball to an open or semi-open player, who possesses no one's gaze until they receive the basketball (too late).

Sneaky and crafty ball distribution is advantageous, partly because the defender of the player receiving the ball is rarely in proper position. When a player is passed to when it's least expected by the defense, they usually don't have a great defense position to prevent scoring, as opposed to their defense positioning in a stagnant or predictable offensive rotation.

Become better passers; teams that average low assist numbers are unsuccessful.

# Types of Passes

Bounce Pass- Effective for fitting the ball in small spaces and capitalizing on opportunities. The receiver of the pass benefits because the ball comes up to them from the floor when they have good positioning and when they only can get to the pass. Another benefit to bounce passes is that less energy is exerted making the pass.

Chest Pass- A pass made at your chest that should land at their chest area. It is easily the most effective and common pass because the ball is moved with minimal effort but puts the receiver in a position that they can make the next effective decision. An efficient chest pass is made with little to no arch during the *route* of the pass. The route of this pass especially should be that of a straight line or close to it. Think of the basketball as a bullet but always with respect to the distance of the receiver.

Overhead Pass- Great for getting the ball to your teammate over defenders' heads. Be sure to have eye contact with the receiver, as you are able to harness a lot of power for the pass. This type of pass covers a nice distance on the court but is not to be overused unless necessary.

One Hand/Baseball Pass- Allows for a quick release of the basketball and can be used with or without a bounce pass. A baseball passes with the basketball is just as it sounds; or try to imagine a quarterback throwing a deep pass to a receiver. Use this pass carefully when making a long down court pass for a fast break or when a team mate is wide open near your team's basket with little-to-no defense opposing him/her.

Behind-the Back/ Wrap Around Pass- Must be practiced before implemented in a live game. More unconventional among the listed basic passing types, but widely used when there is an open recipient and in fast break scenarios. Use with caution, as they are frowned upon if made in error but applauded when successfully executed and resulting in a basket made.

# Tips for Improved Passing

## Strength

A strong and balanced upper body aids the prominent passer. Ideas for improving physical strength for passing include pushups, bench press for adults, planks, and pull ups to name a few. Plainly stated; the stronger the player, the further and stronger the pass.

# Meet the Pass

Develop the habit of stepping to the pass, if necessary, as opposed to waiting for the basketball to land in your hands for a catch. This is extremely irksome from a coach's standpoint and should be discontinued. Appear aggressive by welcoming the basketball and ending the route of the pass early, if possible, especially if it means protecting the ball from being intercepted/deflected.

# Make Eye Contact

Unless your intention is to make an unsuspected assist to someone in scoring position, make sure your pass receiver knows you are likely to pass them the basketball to avoid turnovers. Do not be the basketball player that *throws* the ball *at* their teammates.

# Hockey Assists

Also referred to as, *secondary assists,* they are equally important to grasp for quality offense. Now, passes that lead to the actual assist are tracked in advanced statistics. In Hockey, rather than there being one assist credited for each goal, there's a second assist credited also. Multiple passes are made as diversions before passing to the open player for their goal attempt, thus the assist that led to the assist. As you can imagine, the adoption of the mindset that all passes are important makes for great strategy.

Oscar Robertson, one of the most regarded guards in professional history and an NBA all-time assist leader, suggested you can beat the best players with team efforts, rather than focusing on one opposing superstar.

# Part 3: Defense

*"The best part of basketball for me is getting out there guarding somebody and making them fear me."*- Gary Payton

Consider the following definitions as they pertain to the subject of defense.

Gate- A defensive structure acting as a barrier to outside influence.

Wall- A thing perceived as a protective or restrictive barrier.

Fortress- A person or a thing not susceptible to outside influence or disturbance.

Resistance-The impeding, slowing, or stopping effect exerted by one material thing on another.

# Team Defense

Is the team you are part of steamrolled in efforts to defend their goal? The reasoning behind such a limp disposition is probably due to a few causes:

Lack of defensive technique. Players lack knowledge of defensive positioning, including boxing out, sliding feet, having arms out to cover passing lanes, properly closing out on shot attempts, calling out screens, deflecting/stealing without fouling etc.

Lack of effort. Jogging or walking back on the defensive end of the floor, swiping at the ball handler, or reaching in, rather than sliding their feet, and giving up on the play after a failed attempt at a steal/deflection etc.

Lack of communication. Silence on defense; not asking for help, asking for switches, calling out screens, orchestrating zone or man defense scheme etc.

Lack of pressure/press. Minimal physicality, little-to-no ball pressure upon inbounding, thus allowing offense to advance toward basket resistance free, hands at side, rather than up and out, to discourage pass/shot.

# Individual Defense

Maturing into a sound, man-to-man defender that consistently applies pesky pressure on opponents takes effort and focus over time but can be as rewarding as being *"that player"* on offense. I've seen players make teams, while the coach's decision was based on the player's defensive abilities alone. You may recall that some coaches will maintain starting lineups that include a defensive force, even though they may not be offensive minded, because powerful defenders are invaluable to successful teams. In order to have some type of competitive edge amongst the hordes of players you are in competition with, it behooves you to complete your game and skills set by becoming effective on both ends of the floor, offense *and* defense.

The ability to mentally lock in defensively when necessary does not go unnoticed or unseen, and eventually, defending well does pay off. In fact, many of the greatest offensive players have, for example, been recognized with awards and notation in the history books for their defensive prowess. For many of these professionals, their efforts aided in winning at great heights.

The mind-frame possessed by harsh defenders is that the player they are guarding *will* be *shut down*. Lock down defenders, as such, will take away the offensive player's first choice and force them to do something they are uncomfortable with- pass, use their weak hand or direction, shoot an ill-advised shot, turn the ball over, or have the ball stripped altogether.

There is a certain *pride* that strong defenders are endowed with. Often, they will take responsibility for and/or are assigned to the most prominent scorer on the opposing team. This limits the team's usual success and takes them out of their comfort zone, which actually nudges them to look for other scoring options. The strong-willed defender receives satisfaction from shutting down players and pushing them out of their element. However, they haven't reached staunch defending by accident. They have decided they will add this attribute that pays unending dividends through training diligently, practicing consistently, and studying as they do for their offensive abilities.

# Defensive Tips

Dribbling Pockets- When a basketball is being dribbled, I point out three dribbling pockets, which are the main paths of the basketball as it bounces from the ground to the ball handler's hand. As a defender, be mindful of these three dribbling pockets that are outside the ball handler's left foot, outside their right foot, and the point directly in front of them between their shoes. The ball will be most vulnerable for a steal in these spots, and you may be able to tap the ball in the opposite direction they are headed, as their forward momentum gives you a head start to the ball. A good on-ball defensive habit is using your hand to anticipate the dribble by occupying one of these dribbling pockets. Remember, a good defender will force the ball handler out their comfort zone. It's a pesky annoyance if you take away the first options of your opponent, which typically will involve the ball entering one of these dribbling pockets. For example, imagine yourself in your defensive stance, with one arm dedicated to preventing a low crossover. Crossovers can also be easily stolen as the ball is bouncing up to the other hand of the ball handler, so allow the crossover and wait for the basketball to bounce off the floor and tap it in your direction.

Stay Low-Remember, whoever is lower wins. I've said this applies to both offense and defense. The reason for this is that, in dribbling a ball, the ball must come from the ground, so make the decision that you will have a closer relationship to the ball, even though you don't control it in that instance. Also, consider that the lower you are, the lower your hands can get, and as a rule of thumb, keep in mind that *the steal is low* just as the *block is high* (as in shot block). Good ball handlers will have the awareness to get low to break down a defender, so know when to get low to have as a low center of gravity as they do.

Hands up, Hands out- The idea here is to occupy more space on the court. For example, in a 'ball denial' situation (denying the player you are guarding the possibility of receiving a pass), use your outstretched arm to discourage their teammates from passing them the basketball. They may be able to get free of you with your hands by your side, but if you use your wingspan to cover more space, they will have to work harder to get open for a pass. Try this as an experiment; stand upright, size yourself, and notice your width with your hand out to your side. Now, hold your hands out as if making a letter "T" with your body. Notice that you cover more than three times space as you've made yourself three times as wide. Apply this when necessary on defense and watch how much harder the offense has to work. Imagine the effect when your whole team applies the strategy.

Don't reach-You aren't going to get every steal you go for, but you can increase the number of steals on your stat line by focusing on staying in front of your opponent. What's more important than taking the risk and lunging forward for a steal is cutting off the ball handler's path to the driving lane or the direction they intend to advance. Steals will occur when you notice a weakness or lapse in the ball handler's judgement, and there is your opportunity, but keep quick hands, so you have an easier recovery in case you miss.

Train Defense-Incorporate defense in your workouts as well. Defense requires strong legs, as you'll need to be able to maintain stance for prolonged periods. So, safely strengthen your legs and keep up on your footwork. Don't neglect footwork keenness because acute ball handlers also look at your feet as they handle the ball to get you off-balance and take you off the dribble etc. The more you defend, the better you will defend over time, just like everything else. So, even in pick-up games or in your back yard with your family, play some 'D' on them for practice. After a while, you should be surprised at the amount of playing time you get or success you have during the games, just by stepping up your defensive abilities. For example, if you're trying out for a team and you have other players that are somewhat equivalent to you offensively, try showing your coach that you have a defensive spark and showing the coach you care about defense as much as he/she does. That might give you the edge you need.

Rebounding-The end of a successful defensive stand for a team and an element of defense because rebounding indicates you have caused a missed shot and prevented an additional shot attempt. You may have also gained positioning by boxing out properly to ensure the start of your own offense, which is, of course, substantial. Rebounding should not be under-appreciated.

*"Offense sells tickets, defense wins games, rebounding wins championships."* - Pat Summit

# Part 4:
# Mindset

*"Basketball is Fun."*-Kawhi Leonard

Getting better is simple, not easy, but simple. If you love something, say a sport, you'll dedicate a lot of enjoyable time to that thing. The time spent can lead to being extremely savvy. Your dedication, most likely, will not even feel like work most times because you will simply be spending time doing what you love to do, though others will note the work you've put in. What's more, it is being regarded as gifted, or seeming to *just have it*, as if you were born with it, yet unbeknownst to everyone, you have trained, practiced, and worked on your skills religiously and consistently. You can always tell what a person loves to do. It is usually that which they choose to devote the most time. Fortunately, the more time you spend doing anything, the better you become at it. So, in theory, becoming highly skilled at a certain thing is simple.

In the section of this guide called 'What Is Skill?' the fact is pressed that repetition is the most reliable way to learn a craft, technique, or to form a habit. We've all provided examples of this very real concept that has been around all along. For a simplistic example, all of us had some struggle and frustration with the first attempts at tying our shoes. To this day, the small task of tying our shoes requires no thought to execute. The reason behind such ease is the repetition of the steps and rhythm of tying the shoe laces. There's your evidence; repetition is reliable. Over thousands of trials, repeating the same steps in the same orders, mastery is reached. Make a list of 10 other tasks that are more difficult, that you or someone else seemingly does easily now, yet struggled with at first attempts. It's simple- repeat, repeat, repeat. If it's worth executing to perfection, eventually, repeat thousands of times if you have to. The same can be said about a jump shot or a dribble move. It applies to everything.

# Motivation

Staying motived is a skill in itself. The road to getting to where you want to go in the future is a long one. That said, you will have off-periods and discouragement and, at times, even consider quitting. This is why it is critical to keep motivation close at hand. Ways to stay motivated include, but aren't limited to the following:

Watch or go to a game played by your favorite basketball players, read or learn about their life stories, keep a list of goals and the reasons for achieving them, put up posters in your room of influential athletes or those that are inspirational to you, keep an eye on your competition and their methods, routines, and activities etc.

The above listed can serve as a nail in your heel that pushes the foot forward and a driving motivational force. Here, I list some setbacks you may experience on the way to achieving your goal.

Obstacles will arise. You will get distracted, struggle to find the energy to go out and work on your game. Imperfect conditions, sacrificing what you want right now for what you want most , people will doubt your potential, be intimidated by those that you're in completion with, losing streaks, lack of support, frustration with teammates, insufficient academic status, self-doubt, lack of resources, bad games etc.

With the many speed bumps that arise, you shouldn't hesitate to remind yourself in various ways what you're aiming for. Identify your 'why' -your reason for becoming successful and succeeding at what you do. Once you've established your why, keep it close to your heart and mind, so it can aid you in staying focused. Write your 'why' on paper. Refer to it frequently, daily or weekly, as a reminder, so you can gauge if your activities are bringing you closer or further from achieving your 'why'.

The average person will not be impervious to some of these setbacks and forms of resistance. It's important to understand that you can't put your dreams in the microwave. It doesn't happen overnight. People only see the result; they don't see the work ethic and dedication applied behind the scenes. The individuals you idolize and look up to have likely endured extreme hardships or sacrifice for the realization of their outcome.

# Weaknesses

As well as adding layers onto strengths you have, the importance of finding weak spots in your game and eliminating them or converting them into strengths cannot be stressed enough. The goal is to have very few weak spots in your game and to become that complete player as early as possible and grow in that form. Shortcomings should be identified, i.e., lack of confidence when driving left, the inability to guard the drive to the basket, going up for shots without getting blocked etc. As mentioned previously in this guide, playing one-on-one can reveal your game to you in a helpful light. The same can be said about 2 on 2, 3 on 3, 4 on 4, 5 on 5. I suggest playing it whenever possible, because it serves as a mirror for your progress and highlights areas that need attention.

# Fail

A great deterrent to succeeding is a mental setback, the fear of failing. The fear of failing is known to prevent a person from trying as hard as possible or prevent from trying at all. It has been said that some individuals with the most potential have the least confidence, and those with the less talent have the most confidence, but reach their destinations based on belief and perseverance. This is why we sometimes notice unlikely to succeed individuals and wonder how they came to be in the position they're in. This is because they had fears of failure and self-doubt but tried anyway. Understand that failure is inevitable and a fantastic teacher. Progress eventually blooms from failure and sometimes *only* blooms from failure. Some of basketball's most remembered have missed the most shots but are the most trusted to take the same shots that they have missed. They succeed due to failure. Remember that no one is unerring, and the biggest error is not learning from the mistakes you've made. One must go back to the drawing board to find a solution. Have you noticed that professional teams analyze recorded basketball games to discover ways to improve and prepare for the future? They understand that, if they suffered a loss, it's an opportunity to gain some ground in the right direction.

# Train

The training must be more frequent than the game.

The training must be more challenging than the game.

Over the countless times that you train to transform into a powerful and more skillful athlete; you, your trainer and coach, or whoever you work out with must be of the same sentiment that each training has to be harder than your game might be. Do not spare yourself, as you are readying to be well-equipped in any game situation. A game may call for you to perform through its entirety, and it can be fickle in what it demands. I like to call it being *battle* ready, though the real battle is in the workouts sustained, thus preparing you for times you are on display.

The problem is that, sadly, there are too many that have little to no training. Maybe they do not know how to train at all, but there are others that neglect to train, and know they should do so more often. At the beginning of this guide, I mention the irrational choice to enter a boxing ring or enter combat with a fighter ill-prepared; the notion simply makes no sense. At the same time, wouldn't it be nonsense to get into the ring with a fighter with far less training and combat experience than he or she? You would never do such a thing, as you'd put yourself in danger. What is realistic, though, is matching or surpassing the training and sparring to that of your opponents and future opponents.

The trainings must be more frequent than the games. A conservative ratio is about 4 hours of training and practice for (1) every hour of live competition. The practice I refer to does NOT include team practice. I can sense some of you suggesting that this seems excessive but consider the time that high level football players, for example, spend in the weight room alone. It is not excessive; it's simply what is required as a professional and what you, at a minimum, must consider as an aspiring professional.

# 24 hrs.

The key is having the proper perspective of the 24 hours you have before you. Something I heard very young that stuck with me was to *not underestimate the power of a day.* In truth, your day could be packed with productivity and progress. Your goal should be simply to be better than you were the day before, especially mindful of the myelin insulation around those axons discussed in Part 2 of this guide. Understand the momentum of progress and the skill forming by working on your game day in and day out.

I do understand that you have other things to do throughout your day. However, I like to break the day into categories. If you sleep 8 hours, you have 16 hours to use. Use it wisely. What percentage of your waking day is spent on entertainment (which begs the question- what activities fall under the category of entertainment)? What percent of your day is spent on learning or on education? What percent of your day is spent on improving? If you claim to want to go where you say you do in this lifetime, you have to start assessing your day accordingly. I have players that claim they want to be great as a basketball player, so I follow the statement with, what did you do *today* related to basketball?

Don't be afraid to play basketball 2,3,4 times in one day. The hours of many of your days DO allow for this. You may, for instance, go early in the day to shoot around and put in 100 shots. Go out later that day to train and do some drills. Step outside your door or in front of your garage and work on some ball handling for 10 minutes. Then, in the evening, go play some pickup games for a couple of hours. You may just go work on your jumper several times that day or for several hours that day. You would be surprised how much improvement can be had in 1 day. Then, you wake up the day after, with a new gift of 24 hours in front of you to take advantage of. If you have big plans for yourself and your future, don't get in the habit of wasting these days that you can never have back. If you end up becoming one of the individuals that plays basketball for a living for a while, you WILL be engaging in basketball and other related activities more than once per day to stay in shape and ready to perform.

# Education

To be eligible to play organized basketball, you're going to have to maintain good standing in school. I believe the phrase is, "No books, no ball." For participation in local programs, you're expected to keep your grades above passing level, though I've seen many kids in youth programs able to maintain report cards with a 3.0 and above with relative ease.

You can't be failing in High School and expect to compete at that level. You have to have a balance of school and sports and find a system that works for good study habits. As I mentioned, a small portion of good players make it to the next level. One of the reasons behind this fallout is the athlete's lack of focus or concern in the classroom. Unfortunately, there are many talented basketball players that are academically ineligible to show what they can do.

To go to college and play sports, the requirements are as follows:

High school graduate

Pass 16 core courses with at least a 2.0 GPA

Score well on SAT or ACT

Beyond going to school and then college for the purpose of playing basketball, you should also tie schooling to being the most you can be and developing into a well-rounded and intelligent individual. Doing so will aid you in life after basketball -and there is an after basketball- tremendously.

# You

The fact is that you are a human being, and you are capable of far more than you think you are right now. Also, the fact remains that there is no limit to your creativity, and the rest of us should have to brace ourselves for the impact of your self-expression. In the end, basketball is a game, and a basketball is a toy. You can do more with it than you are presently aware. If you love basketball, prove it and play it every day. Your fellow human beings in the past and today will have achieved extraordinary things, some far more substantial than anything in the realm of basketball, which is why you should approach the day with enthusiasm, because every day is a chance to turn things around. Get to work.

# Part 5
# Diagrams and Training Tools

## Training Tools

Here's a list of optional training tools you can utilize when applicable to your workouts.

Basketball

Jump Rope

Tennis Ball

Weighted Trainer ball or "Heavy Ball"

Blindfold

Dribble Glasses

Oversized Ball

Ball Wrap/Plastic Bag

Weight Vest

Speed Ladder

Training Cones

Notepad and Pen

Medicine Ball

Game Ball

Coach's Dry Erase Board

Referee Handbook

# Basketball Diagrams

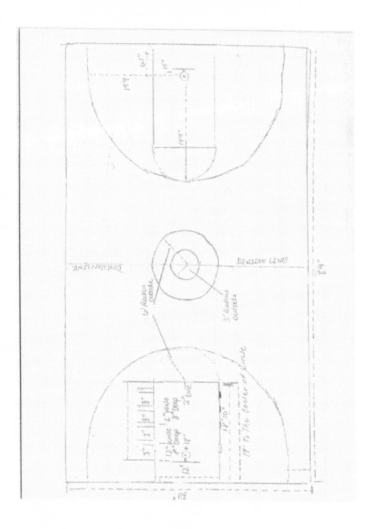

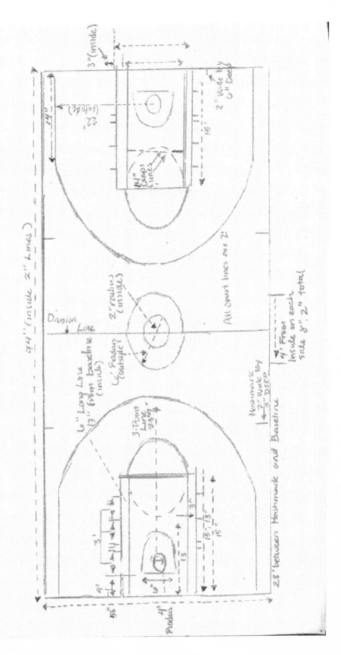

94" (inside 2" lines)

3" (inside)

2" Wide on Deep

(inside)
23"

18"

Baker
Line

Division Line

2" radius (inside)

6' Radius (outside)

All court lines are 2"

4" From inside on each side 8" 2" total

6" Long Line 13" From Baseline (inside)

3-Point Line 23'9"

Hashmark 2" Wide by 3" Deep

3"

18'-3½" 15"

3'

3'

4'

4'

50'

Radius

28' between Hashmark and Baseline

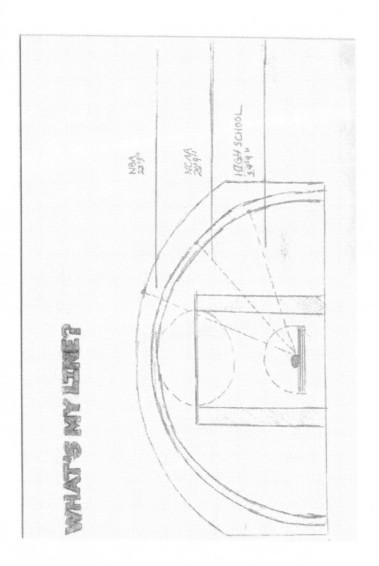
WHAT'S MY LINE?

NBA
23'9"

NCAA
20'9"

HIGH SCHOOL
19'9"

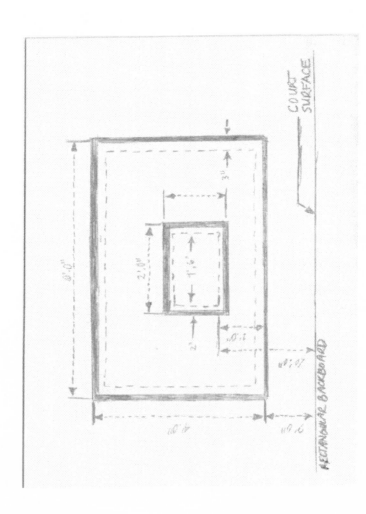

RECTANGULAR BACKBOARD

COURT SURFACE

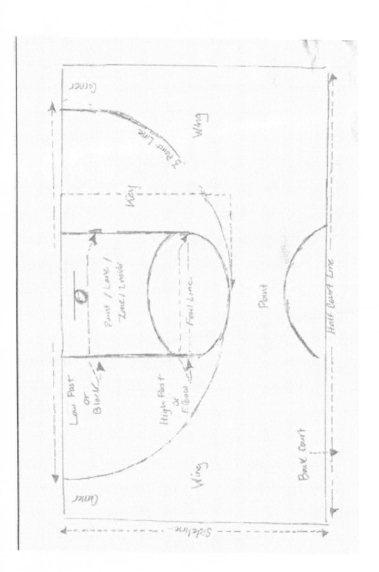

Corner

Wing

3 Point Line

Key

Low Post or Block

High Post or Elbow

Point / Lane / Zone / Inside

Foul Line

Point

Half Court Line

Back Court

Wing

Corner

Sideline

Diagram of 2 regulation size basketballs squeezed to fit inside of regulation size rim.

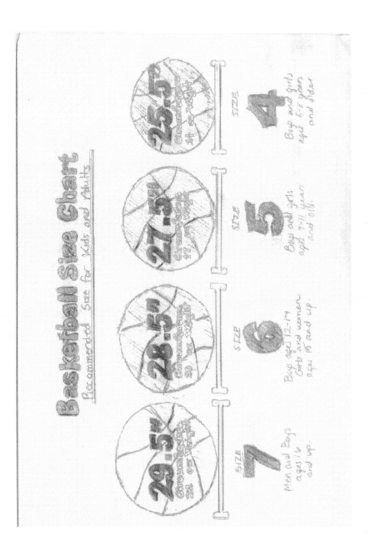

Made in the USA
Columbia, SC
16 March 2020